THE WAR IN VIETNAM

THE WAR IN VIETNAM

BY DON LAWSON

A GROLIER COMPANY

A FIRST BOOK
FRANKLIN WATTS
NEW YORK | LONDON | TORONTO | 1981

Cover photograph courtesy of United Press International

Photographs courtesy of United Press International: pp.
ii, 6, 17, 19, 36, 43, 47, 52, 66, 68; U.S. Air Force: p.
20; U.S. Navy: pp. 25, 28; Derk Maitland: p. 33; Army
News Features: p. 38; U.S. Army: p. 44; Lyndon B. Johnson Library: p. 55.

Map by Vantage Art, Inc.

Library of Congress Cataloging in Publication Data

Lawson, Don.
    The war in Vietnam.

    (A First book)
    Bibliography: p.
    Includes index.
    Summary: Describes events leading to war in Viet-
nam, American involvement, opposition at home, the end
of the conflict, and the aftermath of the war.
    1. Vietnamese Conflict, 1961–1975—Juvenile litera-
ture. [1. Vietnamese Conflict, 1961–1975] I. Title.
DS557.7.L38   959.704′3   81–3064
ISBN 0–531–04331–2   AACR2

CONTENTS

THE WAR IN VIETNAM

PLAYING DOMINOES
WITH COUNTRIES

In the sport of bowling, if all ten pins in an alley are knocked down by rolling a single ball into them, it is not the ball that does all the work. It just starts the job. The ball knocks down several pins that in turn fly into the other pins and knock them down.

A similar chain reaction takes place in knocking down a row of dominoes. If a number of dominoes are set on end in a row and the first domino is toppled, it will fall against the second domino and topple it, and so on right down the line until the entire row has been knocked down.

The main difference between the falling pins and the falling dominoes is that many of the pins fall at the same time, while the dominoes topple over one at a time. Interestingly, it was because many U.S. leaders thought of several of the countries in Southeast Asia as a row of dominoes that the United States got into the Vietnam War.

It was President Dwight David "Ike" Eisenhower who first put this idea into words. On April 7, 1954, he said that all of Southeast Asia was like a row of dominoes. "You knock over the first one, and the last one will go over very quickly." This soon became known as the Domino Theory in world affairs.

The country that Eisenhower feared was going to start toppling over nations in Southeast Asia was Communist Russia. He did not think Russia would itself make the first move. Instead, it would support local Communist efforts to gain control of a particular country. If these efforts succeeded, Russia would then move in and take charge. This domino effect

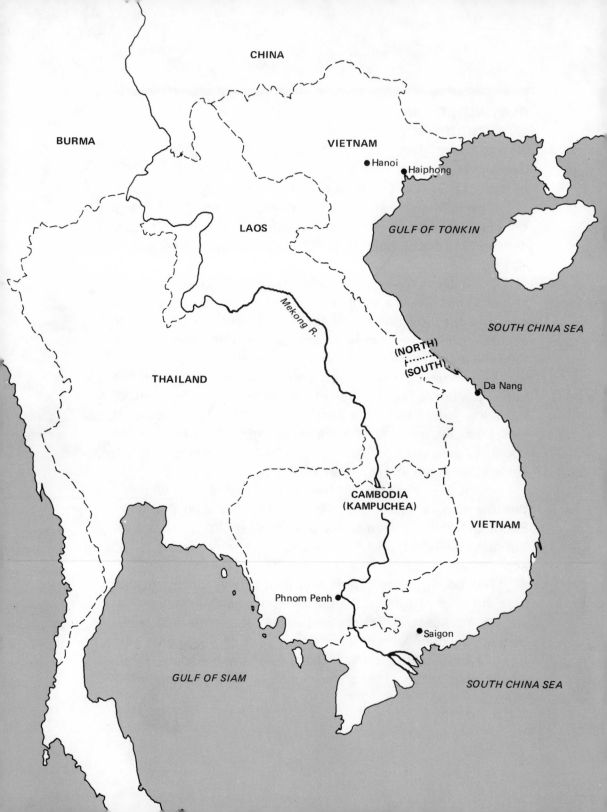

would then be used to take over neighboring countries until all of Southeast Asia was under Russian control.

Eisenhower believed that Vietnam was being threatened by just such a Communist take-over. If Vietnam fell, he and other U.S. leaders feared that Vietnam's neighbors, Laos, Cambodia, and Thailand, would also soon topple over. Before long the whole area would be under Communist control, which the United States did not want to happen. The United States wanted all of the countries of Southeast Asia to be independent, to choose their own leaders and their own forms of government.

THE FRENCH IN INDOCHINA

For many years before World War II the countries now known as Vietnam, Laos, and Cambodia or Kampuchea were controlled by France. They were a part of France's huge overseas colonial empire. The peninsula in Southeast Asia occupied by these countries was called French Indochina. French Indochina was rich in rice, rubber, minerals, silk, and other valuable products. The money from the export and sale of these products helped make France rich. But the people of French Indochina got relatively little of this money. They remained poor peasants even though it was their country and their work that produced the vast wealth resulting from the sale of Indochinese exports.

The people of Indochina resented being taken advantage of by the French. But for a long time there was not much they could do about it. France was a powerful military country. It could easily put down any attempts at revolt against French colonial rule. In addition, France did try to keep the Indochinese people happy by improving their living conditions.

Good school systems were established, health care was improved, and good food and clothing were made available to all.

Nevertheless, Indochina was governed by the French as if they owned it, and the Indochinese had very little to say about their own affairs. The anger of the Indochinese at their own lack of independence smoldered like a half-smothered fire. It threatened to break into flame at any time.

France, of course, was not the only European nation with an overseas empire. Many other nations of the world also had them—Great Britain, the Netherlands, Belgium, Portugal, and several more. These empires were all run the same way. The country in charge took advantage of or exploited the countries under its control for its own purposes. Great Britain, for example, had a huge overseas empire. The profits from colonial India alone made Britain a wealthy nation and a world power.

One of the few major nations without such an overseas empire was the United States. A part of the reason for this was that the United States had so much natural wealth of its own that it did not need to exploit other nations. More importantly, however, the United States itself had once been a colony of Great Britain. Ever since America's own successful fight for independence in the American Revolution, its people were unsympathetic toward colonial empires.

BREAK-UP OF
THE COLONIAL EMPIRES
One of the most important things accomplished by World War II was the worldwide break-up of most of the overseas colonial empires. Great Britain led the way. Not only did it return to the people of such nations as India their independence, but it also taught them how to govern themselves.

4

France, however, tried to regain the empire it had lost during the war. In Africa, France fought long and bloody battles against Algerians who were willing to fight and die for their independence. And in Indochina the French tried to re-occupy and re-establish the key to their Southeast Asian overseas empire in Vietnam.

During World War II, Vietnam had been occupied by the Japanese. Toward the end of the war, Allied forces drove out the Japanese. This left a kind of vacuum as far as control of Vietnam was concerned. It was into this vacuum that France tried to move soon after World War II ended.

REVOLUTIONARY LEADER
HO CHI MINH

But like the Algerians, the Vietnamese had now stubbornly set their minds and hearts on independence. Their leader was a fiery revolutionary named Ho Chi Minh. The organization that Ho Chi Minh headed was called the Vietminh, or Vietnam Independence League. On September 2, 1945, the Vietminh established a new independent government called the Democratic Republic of Vietnam (DRV). Its headquarters were in Hanoi in North Vietnam. It was this government that the French tried to overthrow when they moved back into Indochina at the end of 1945. Warfare between the French and the Vietminh broke out the following year.

The French and almost everybody else thought that the badly outnumbered and poorly equipped Vietminh would be quickly defeated. But they forgot about two things: the burning desire of the Vietnamese people for independence, and the military genius of the Vietminh's top general, Vo Nguyen Giap.

Giap was a genius at guerrilla warfare, a kind of fighting

5

in which surprise attacks against the enemy are made with small bands of warriors. The guerrillas suddenly appeared out of the forest or jungle, struck their lethal blows, and disappeared again as swiftly, as silently as they had come. They left behind them dead, wounded, and thoroughly confused survivors who did not quite know what struck them or from where.

Sometimes Giap's guerrillas would act as snipers. They would lie hidden in villages or near a jungle trail and then pick off a column of advancing French troops one man at a time. Sniper attacks, surprise ambushes, and night attacks on sleeping troops steadily drained away the French troops' will to fight. And such warfare threatened to go on for years unless the Vietminh could be forced to "come out and fight" in regular face-to-face battles. But General Giap and his guerrillas refused to do this.

By the early 1950s the French had become completely and hopelessly bogged down in what seemed like an endless effort to regain control of Vietnam. They did control most of the larger towns and cities in South Vietnam. But Giap's guerrillas still controlled the rural countryside. This made it impossible for the French to travel between cities except by air. It was at this point that the United States under President Eisenhower began to give major help to the French in their battle against the Vietminh.

THE KOREAN WAR
President Eisenhower wasn't the first or the only American leader to think that Russia was trying to topple over countries

Ho Chi Minh

like dominoes. He was just the first person to put the Domino Theory into words. Harry S. Truman, who was President before Eisenhower, also feared the Russians. And the American State and Defense Departments even issued a joint statement during Truman's term in office that said, "The Soviet Union . . . seeks to impose its absolute authority over the rest of the world."

President Truman and the State and Defense Departments had good reason for fearing Soviet plans in certain parts of Southeast Asia other than Vietnam. In 1950, Communist North Korea had tried to take over the Republic of South Korea. North Korea was aided by Communist Russia and Communist China in this attack. At the end of World War II the United Nations had been formed to prevent just such so-called "Acts of Aggression." When South Korea was invaded, the United States and other United Nations members immediately went to South Korea's aid and an undeclared war began.

During the Korean War, President Truman also gave U.S. military aid to the French in Vietnam. He did so because Ho Chi Minh and his Vietminh government were now accepting Communist military aid from both China and the Soviet Union. What may have started out as a revolutionary fight for independence by the Vietminh now looked to Truman like a typical Communist take-over of yet another country.

Like the French-Vietnamese conflict in Indochina, the Korean conflict looked as if it might drag on indefinitely. But when Eisenhower became President in 1953, he was able to arrange a truce in the Korean conflict. Eisenhower had been the commanding general who led the Allied armies to victory over Germany and Italy in Europe during World War II. He was now determined that the United States should not take part in any more wars. As a result he was dead set against sending any more American troops to fight in Southeast Asia where a war might be endless.

Nevertheless, Eisenhower did fear continued Communist conquest in Southeast Asia, as he made clear in his Domino Theory statement. And now that China and Russia were both openly supporting the North Vietnamese, he feared a Communist take-over in Indochina just as much as Truman had. Consequently, Eisenhower and his Secretary of State, John Foster Dulles, led the U.S. government in continuing to give money and military supplies to the French in Vietnam.

THE BATTLE OF
DIEN BIEN PHU

The struggle for control of Vietnam between the French and the Vietminh forces came to a head at the village of Dien Bien Phu in North Vietnam in the spring of 1954. Here, in a battle that some historians have called one of the most important battles in the history of the world, the French were finally driven out of Indochina.

Several French generals had tried unsuccessfully for years to force General Giap's guerrillas into a big face-to-face battle. The French generals were convinced that in such a fight Giap's army could be totally defeated and the French would thus win the war. But Giap's forces had always refused to engage in such a battle. Why should they when their guerrilla warfare had all but defeated the French up to now?

It was French General Henri Navarre who thought he finally had a way to get all of Giap's guerrillas to stand still and fight in one place at one time. Navarre's idea was to set a trap. He would bring together almost all of the French army in Vietnam in a place where it looked like it could easily be

9

attacked and defeated. This would tempt the Vietminh into also bringing their troops together to attack the French. Once such a battle began, Navarre believed, his troops would win.

Navarre did not simply think that the French soldiers were better fighters than the Vietnamese. He was too experienced a soldier to believe that. But he was convinced that the Vietnamese could not continue to supply a single, large combat force with food and ammunition for a long battle. The French, on the other hand, could bring in such supplies by air. Since the French had a number of transport aircraft, many of which were American, and the Vietnamese had none, the outcome in favor of the French seemed certain.

The village of Dien Bien Phu was in a valley in North Vietnam near the border of Laos. Here the French set up their defensive positions and waited for the Vietminh to attack. In a normal battle the hills surrounding the camp would have been a disadvantage for the French. The enemy might place big artillery guns on top of them and fire down into the French camp. But General Navarre did not think that the Vietminh had enough such heavy artillery to do this. There were about 16,000 French troops in the camp. Many of them were members of the famous French Foreign Legion who were among the best fighters in the world. Navarre did not know how many men General Giap would be able to gather together to attack Dien Bien Phu. When Navarre's intelligence officers told him that Giap planned on using 50,000 Vietminh in the attack, Navarre laughed in disbelief.

The battle opened on March 13, 1954, and General Navarre was immediately proved wrong on all counts. First of all, the Vietminh had indeed placed a number of big guns in the surrounding hills. These guns opened the battle with a fierce bombardment that all but left the French camp in ruins. Secondly, there were indeed some 50,000 Vietminh surrounding the French. And finally, Giap's army was never in danger of running out of supplies.

General Giap had asked for the help of thousands of Vietnamese peasants to act as load-carrying porters, and Ho Chi Minh had rallied much of the North Vietnamese population to Giap's aid. Each peasant carried a huge bag of rice or dried fish or ammunition on his or her back to supply the soldiers. Some peasants even pushed specially built bicycles that could carry several hundred pounds of supplies along the jungle trails. Usually this great human supply train traveled only by night. But even when it moved by day, the thick roof of jungle trees hid it from the French fighter and bomber pilots flying overhead.

But the French were veteran fighters. They were shocked by the opening artillery bombardment, but they were not swept off their feet when the Vietminh ground forces attacked. Led by the Legionnaires, the French rallied their forces and fought off the assault. Casualties ran high on both sides.

Soon the battle of Dien Bien Phu settled into a siege with neither side able to gain the advantage. But day by day the Vietminh narrowed their circle surrounding the camp. The two colonels in charge of the French radioed Saigon for reinforcements by air, but the artillery bombardment had destroyed the small airfield runway. A few reinforcements as well as supplies were parachuted in.

When the siege had lasted for several weeks and it looked like defeat was certain, the French government in Paris asked the United States government in Washington for more extensive military aid. Aerial bombardment from planes based on U.S. Navy aircraft carriers in the nearby South China Sea might blunt the Vietminh attack.

There were some high officials in Washington who were in favor of such direct military aid to the French. Secretary of State Dulles was one. There was even some talk of using atomic bombs in such a bombardment. But President Eisenhower disagreed. Such aid would mean exactly the kind of involvement he was trying to avoid. The request was refused, and the French were left no choice but to fight on alone.

THE ANGEL OF DIEN BIEN PHU

Despite the fact that the end of the battle always seemed near, the French held out through April. Taking care of their casualties became one of the defenders' most serious problems. At the beginning of the battle a small hospital had been set up with a lone French doctor, Major Paul Grauwin, in charge. He was assisted by a heroic nurse, Genevieve de Galard-Terraube. The only woman in the French camp, she was called "The Angel of Dien Bien Phu."

It had been thought before the battle began that casualties would be airlifted out of the French camp to a hospital in Saigon. But the battered airstrip prevented such aerial evacuation of the wounded. Dr. Grauwin and nurse Galard-Terraube had to try to take care of several thousand wounded with the help of only a few aides. Both the heroic doctor and nurse lived through the siege and were later awarded France's highest military honors.

During the first week in May, the Vietminh finally overran the French camp. General Giap had offered the French an opportunity to surrender, but they refused. Still led by the

Legionnaires, the French fought on until they were overwhelmed in hand-to-hand combat. Only a few thousand of the original force of 16,000 French defenders of Dien Bien Phu were left to be captured. They were marched off to Vietnamese prison camps. Along the way many more French soldiers died. Those who remained were later released and returned to France.

PEACE CONFERENCE
LEADS TO WAR

Many nations were afraid that any more fighting in Southeast Asia might lead to World War III. A peace conference was held at Geneva, Switzerland, soon after the French were driven from Vietnam to try to prevent this. Most of the major nations of the world attended the conference. The smaller nations of Indochina also sent delegates.

One of the things decided at the Geneva peace conference was to divide Vietnam into two parts, North and South Vietnam. An imaginary dividing line was drawn across the middle of the country. The area north of this line was to belong to Ho Chi Minh's government. The area south of the dividing line was to belong to the Republic of Vietnam.

No military troops from either side were allowed to occupy a narrow strip of land on either side of the imaginary line dividing the country. This area was called the Demilitarized Zone, or DMZ.

The division of Vietnam into North and South Vietnam was originally intended to be temporary. The Vietnamese on both sides of the DMZ agreed that elections would be held within two years. These elections were intended to re-unite the country and to decide who would run it.

THE UNITED STATES
BACKS SOUTH VIETNAM
The United States did not want the Communist government of North Vietnam to take control of the whole country. To keep this from happening the United States decided to support

South Vietnam. This support, the United States said, would only be given until the free elections to unite the country were held.

As soon as Vietnam was officially divided into two countries, hundreds of thousands of people began to flee from North Vietnam into South Vietnam. Many fled in fear. Ho Chi Minh had promised to divide all of North Vietnam's farms equally among all of the people. To do this, large farms were taken away from their owners. These large landowners were threatened with death or imprisonment if they did not give up their farms willingly. Thousands of stubborn landowners were killed in this program.

Thousands of other North Vietnamese crossed the DMZ and fled into South Vietnam because that was where the best farmland was. Most of the country's food had been grown in South Vietnam's "rice bowl" at the mouth of the Mekong River. But when more than a million North Vietnamese refugees flooded into South Vietnam, there were serious food shortages. To help solve this problem, President Eisenhower ordered that increased economic aid be given to the South Vietnamese government.

Eisenhower also had several hundred military men sent to South Vietnam. These soldiers were called "military advisers." They were supposed to help train and give advice to the South Vietnamese army. This army numbered about 150,000 men, but they were not well trained. President Eisenhower was afraid that General Giap's highly trained North Vietnamese army might decide to cross the DMZ and try to take control of South Vietnam by force. He wanted to be sure that the South Vietnamese army was ready to fight off such a threat. The South Vietnamese army was also equipped with modern American weapons and other military equipment.

THE VIETCONG

North Vietnam actually had two armies. One was made up of General Giap's veteran Vietminh regulars north of the DMZ. The other was made up of Vietminh who remained in South Vietnam after the country was divided. They were called the Vietcong, which means "Vietnamese Communists."

For several years after the division of Vietnam, the Vietcong were a kind of secret army in South Vietnam. They carried on guerrilla warfare against the South Vietnamese government. In time they were joined by General Giap's northern guerrillas who made raids across the DMZ. Together the two forces were known as the National Liberation Army or National Liberation Front.

North Vietnamese fighting forces were often called the Vietcong or simply VC by American soldiers. But in addition to the Vietcong guerrillas fighting in the south, North Vietnam always had its own separate regular army that usually stayed north of the DMZ. The two forces together numbered several hundred thousand men.

DICTATOR DIEM

After it was agreed at Geneva that South Vietnam should become a democratic republic, a new President of the Republic of Vietnam was also agreed upon, named Ngo Dinh Diem. Diem refused to let South Vietnam take part in the free general elections throughout the country that had been agreed to at Geneva. He refused, he said, because honest free elections were not possible in North Vietnam while it was

Ngo Dinh Diem

controlled by the Communists. Actually Diem was afraid that such elections would result in his being voted out of office.

Diem was a dictator. He promised the people of South Vietnam freedom and equality but never lived up to his promises. Bribery and corruption were common throughout his administration. Important government jobs and special favors were given to people who had the money to pay for them. In addition, Diem saw to it that many members of his family were given key government positions and paid high salaries.

Despite Diem's failure as a democratic leader, the United States continued to support him. One reason was that Diem was an outspoken foe of Communism. Some U.S. officials feared that if Diem were overthrown a leader sympathetic to Communism might be elected in his place.

United States support of Diem continued even after John F. Kennedy succeeded Eisenhower as President in 1961. Although there still had been no free elections in Vietnam, Kennedy's administration continued to support dictator Diem with more economic aid and more military advisers. There were 2,000 U.S. military advisers in South Vietnam when Eisenhower left office. Under President Kennedy this number soon swelled to some 15,000.

KENNEDY AND
THE GREEN BERETS

Many of the military advisers sent to Vietnam under President Kennedy were members of what the U.S. Army called "Special Forces." Trained in guerrilla warfare to fight against guerrillas, they soon became known as the "Green Berets," because of the green berets they wore on which was pinned a badge that identified their branch of service.

Green Berets were not actually supposed to fight against

*An American "adviser" in Vietnam, on
patrol duty near the Cambodian border.*

*Paratroopers are dropped into a
remote mountain area in North Vietnam.*

the Vietcong. To do so could mean that the United States was officially at war against North Vietnam. Like all U.S. military advisers in South Vietnam, the Green Berets were just supposed to give advice to the Army of the Republic of Vietnam (ARVN). But when the Green Berets went with ARVN troops into battle against the Vietcong they usually took part in the fighting. The first U.S. soldier to be killed in Vietnam was a Green Beret. He was James T. Davis from Tennessee. Davis, 25, was killed in action against the Vietcong in December 1961, several years before the United States "officially" entered the war.

The Vietcong soon discovered that the Green Berets were fierce fighters. Not only were they skilled in jungle warfare, but they also were experts at hit-and-run guerrilla attacks. Since they were trained as paratroopers, the Green Berets could also be parachuted into remote jungle and mountain areas where the Vietcong were hiding. Surprise attacks on these Vietcong hideouts often kept the Vietcong from attacking South Vietnamese towns and cities.

When he first took office, President Kennedy thought that regular U.S. Army infantry troops might have to be sent to South Vietnam to keep Diem's government from being overthrown. But Kennedy hesitated to make such a move because he agreed with Eisenhower that the United States should not get involved in a major ground war in Southeast Asia. The success of the Green Berets in their secret war against the Vietcong gave Kennedy an answer to his problem. More and more Green Berets were sent to Vietnam.

THE ASSASSINATION
OF DIEM

But the Vietcong were not South Vietnam's only problem. Nor were they President Kennedy's only problem in dealing with

South Vietnam's Diem regime. The main problem seemed to be Diem himself.

Kennedy soon discovered that Diem was as unpopular with his own people in South Vietnam as he was with the North Vietnamese. One of the things that made Diem unpopular was his refusal to let certain religious groups worship freely. Diem was a Roman Catholic, and he frowned on other religions, especially Buddhism. Buddhism is a widespread Asian religion whose followers believe in a quiet, peaceful way of life. Through silent worship and self-denial they hope to find the true meaning of life.

In the spring of 1963, Buddhists throughout South Vietnam planned to celebrate the birthday of the man who had founded their religion, Gautama Buddha. Diem ordered ARVN troops to put a stop to these celebrations. The result was widespread riots. And in South Vietnam's capital, Saigon, several Buddhist priests protested by setting gasoline-soaked robes they were wearing on fire and burning themselves to death. ARVN troops managed to put down the riots, but the protests continued for days.

When word of what was happening in South Vietnam reached the United States, President Kennedy was furious. A Catholic himself, Kennedy had no patience for any leader who did not let his people practice whatever religion they wanted. Kennedy immediately sent word to Diem that he must announce a national policy of religious freedom for all South Vietnamese or the United States would withdraw all of its economic and military support.

Diem quickly agreed to Kennedy's demands, but the unrest continued. The Vietcong also took advantage of the situation by attacking towns and cities throughout South Vietnam, including Saigon. Scattered fighting went on throughout the summer.

In early November, a group of ARVN generals decided they had had enough of the Diem regime. They feared that if Diem continued in office any longer the people of South Vietnam would revolt and, aided by the Vietcong, take over the government. This group of dissatisfied generals took Diem from the Presidential Palace in Saigon and killed him. The generals themselves then took charge of running the country.

The assassination of Diem was not the only violent act to occur in that grim November of 1963. Later in the month, on November 22, President Kennedy was killed by an assassin in Dallas, Texas, during a parade.

PRESIDENT JOHNSON
TAKES COMMAND

The man who succeeded Kennedy as President was a native Texan and had been in the parade with Kennedy on the fatal trip. He was Lyndon Baines Johnson, who had been Vice President under the slain Chief Executive. Although he did not want the United States to become entangled in a war in Vietnam, it was Johnson who first sent large numbers of military forces there.

But to begin with President Johnson told the new South Vietnamese President, General Nguyen Khanh, that the South Vietnamese Army would have to be made strong enough to defend South Vietnam by itself. Khanh agreed that this was possible, but to build up his ARVN forces he would need much more money. President Johnson approved $60 million in additional aid.

For a time, Khanh went through the motions of strengthening his army, but then he began to demand that the United States use American military forces to attack North Vietnam. Unless this was done, Khanh said, the Vietcong would soon overrun South Vietnam.

President Johnson was now caught in a trap. Like the several Presidents before him, Johnson feared a Communist take-over in Indochina. Johnson's aides told him that Vietcong forces were already in control of much of South Vietnam. If the United States backed out now, it would mean an American defeat and a Communist victory. Johnson's solution to the problem was to expand the secret use of American military forces against the Vietcong.

In addition to the Green Berets, American pilots now also joined the action. They flew the planes that parachuted Green Berets into Vietcong territory. They also flew observation missions. And beginning in 1964 they began to take part in secret bombing missions. The North Vietnamese, of course, were aware of this growing American military activity. It was only the American people who were unaware of it.

It was the use of the U.S. Navy that finally brought the United States completely into the war.

THE GULF OF TONKIN INCIDENT

During the summer of 1964 two United States Navy destroyers were sent into the Gulf of Tonkin just off the coast of North Vietnam. The destroyers were the *Maddox* and the *C. Turner Joy.* Officially the destroyers were on patrol duty. Actually they were gathering military information. Their job was to learn the locations of North Vietnamese radar towers and naval bases. Radar was used to detect any planes that might fly in to attack the naval bases. If the radar towers could be located, either ARVN or American forces could later put them out of action.

On August 4, while the *Maddox* and *C. Turner Joy* were on "patrol duty" in the Gulf of Tonkin, they were attacked by

This photograph was taken from aboard the U.S. destroyer Maddox *during the August 4 Gulf of Tonkin ''attack'' on American ships.*

North Vietnamese patrol, or PT, gunboats. Or at least that was what the captains and crews of the destroyers apparently thought had happened. Later there was serious doubt about whether the *Maddox* and *C. Turner Joy* had been attacked at all. Neither destroyer was damaged and there were no U.S. casualties.

When word of the "attack" reached Washington, President Johnson acted immediately. Now U.S. military action would no longer have to be conducted in secret. The President, as Commander in Chief of all U.S. military forces, immediately ordered American bombing planes to fly from aircraft carriers in the Gulf of Tonkin and bomb North Vietnamese naval bases.

Johnson also went before the U.S. Congress and asked for authority to take additional action if it proved necessary. Johnson did not ask for a declaration of war. He was certain that a request for a declaration of war would be defeated. But his request to widen the war, he thought, would pass Congress easily. Johnson was right.

On August 7, Congress passed the Gulf of Tonkin Resolution which had the same effect as a declaration of war. It authorized President Johnson "to take all necessary measures to repel any armed attacks against the forces of the United States." It also authorized him "to take all necessary steps including the use of armed force to assist South Vietnam." The United States was now at war against North Vietnam.

AMERICAN WARFARE AGAINST THE VIETCONG AND NORTH VIETNAM

Lyndon Johnson did not want to be a wartime President. More than anything else he wanted to be a great peacetime President. He had big dreams for America. These dreams could only come true if the country were at peace. But neither did Johnson want to be the first man to be President when the United States lost a war. What he decided had to be done now was to win the Vietnam War quickly. Then he could get back to the truly important job of guiding a peaceful America toward what he called a "Great Society."

Johnson thought that the way to end the war quickly was by aerial bombardment. North Vietnam had only a small air force. What few planes it had could probably be easily knocked out of the skies by American-trained South Vietnamese fighter pilots flying American-built fighter planes. And if the South Vietnamese couldn't do the job, American fighter pilots could. Then American bombers could bomb North Vietnam at will. This, President Johnson believed, would force Ho Chi Minh to ask for peace.

An air war had one great advantage as far as President Johnson and the American people were concerned. It seemed like a "clean" war. No American soldiers would be killed in bloody ground combat. And Johnson promised the American people that he was not going to send American boys "to do the job Asian boys ought to be doing for themselves." The pilots dropping the bombs, of course, did not see the death and destruction the bombs caused. Nor did the American people.

27

*U.S. bombers launched massive air attacks
against North Vietnam throughout the war.*

Nevertheless, on the strength of his promise to keep the United States out of the war, Lyndon Johnson was re-elected President on November 3, 1964. He defeated Arizona Senator Barry Goldwater. People feared that if Goldwater were elected he might get the United States into a nuclear war.

OPERATION ROLLING THUNDER

Aerial warfare against North Vietnam began on a small scale. Bridges and supply routes were attacked in an attempt to cut off food and ammunition being carried from North Vietnam to the Vietcong in South Vietnam. The main supply route was called the Ho Chi Minh Trail. It ran from north of the DMZ, through a part of neighboring Laos, and on down into South Vietnam. But all attempts to stop the flow of supplies along this trail were only temporarily successful. Within a matter of hours after each aerial bombardment peasant porters were once again moving along the Ho Chi Minh Trail carrying their vital cargo to the Vietcong.

Elsewhere, the early American air raids were equally unsuccessful. The Vietcong continued to launch guerrilla raids against towns and cities throughout South Vietnam. In fact there was one such raid against the American Embassy in Saigon. In response to this last attack Johnson decided to launch an aerial offensive against North Vietnam. It was called "Operation Rolling Thunder." Its purpose was to force Ho Chi Minh to ask for peace.

Operation Rolling Thunder was begun in the spring of 1965. With brief halts it was to last until late in 1968. The pauses were to see if Ho Chi Minh wanted to say anything about stopping the war. But the only thing the North Vietnamese leader said was that he wanted the Americans to get out of Vietnam. Then he would be willing to talk peace.

29

THE MARINES LAND
AT DA NANG

In order to launch Operation Rolling Thunder, several large U.S. airfields had to be built in South Vietnam. The largest of these was at Da Nang. To protect the Da Nang airfield, a brigade of U.S. Marines was landed there on March 5, 1965. Several weeks later a U.S. Army airborne brigade was also landed in South Vietnam.

By late July President Johnson no longer tried to pretend that the war could be won without sending American troops into combat. On July 28 Johnson told a televised press conference: "I have today ordered to Vietnam the 1st Cavalry Airmobile Division and certain other forces, which will raise our fighting strength to almost 125,000 men. Additional forces," the President added, "will be needed, and they will be sent as requested."

To say the least, the American public was startled by Johnson's announcement. Up to now few people had realized how deeply the United States had become involved in the Vietnam War. Before the year ended there would be some 200,000 U.S. soldiers in Vietnam, and the number would continue to grow. So would the number of American casualties.

FIGHTING THE
VIETCONG GUERRILLAS

As the French and the Green Berets had already discovered, Giap's guerrillas and the Vietcong did not fight according to western "rules." Now it was the U.S. Army and Marine infantrymen who were forced to learn this grim lesson.

Unlike the Green Berets, few of the U.S. Army and Marine infantrymen or their officers knew much about guerrilla warfare. Not many had even had any combat experience of any kind. Some had fought in the Korean War and in World War II. But in those wars the enemy had rarely used guerrilla methods.

United States enlisted ground troops in Vietnam called themselves "grunts." They were no less brave than the American "doughboys," "dogfaces," and "G.I.s" of World War I, World War II, and the Korean War. In fact in many ways they were even more heroic, because the grunts constantly faced death in the jungle against an enemy they seldom saw. In addition, they were all too often led by officers just out of school with no combat experience who did everything "by the book."

The grunts called the Vietcong enemy "Victor Charlie" (for VC) or just "Charlie." When they first saw Charlie he did not look like much of a soldier. He was dressed in a ragged uniform that looked like black silk pajamas. On his feet he wore sandals that were often cut from old truck tires. But Charlie was as tough and vicious a fighting man as any American soldier had ever faced. He never panicked under fire. And he did not hesitate to use whatever weapons that were available to kill grunts or ARVN soldiers.

THE FLYING MUD BOMB
AND PUNJI STAKES

One of the primitive weapons that Charlie used and one that the grunts feared the most was called "the flying mud bomb" or "flying mace." It could hack a jungle patrol to pieces in one silent swing of a long rope.

The bomb was made by packing a wicker basket with 500 pounds (225 kg) of mud. Through the mud were run dozens of razor-sharp bamboo stakes with their points sticking out on all sides. When it dried, the mud bomb was suspended at the end of a rope or vine above a jungle trail. A wire was hidden on the ground to trip or trigger the release of the suspended mud ball. When the leader of a patrol stumbled over this trip wire, down swung the spinning, spiked ball cutting down everything in its path.

The sharpened bamboo, or "punji" stakes were also used as silent killers in other ways. Pits were dug in jungle trails, and their floors were lined with the bamboo spikes. The pits were then covered over with tree branches and leaves. Unwary patrols often stumbled into such hidden pits or booby traps and were killed before they knew what had happened. Before the war such pits had been used to capture and kill wild animals.

Punji stakes were also planted in rice fields or paddies. They could not be seen because the paddies were covered by several inches of water. To avoid jungle booby traps grunts sometimes waded across the open rice paddies. If they stepped on a punji stake, they could be put out of action for weeks.

OTHER VIETCONG WEAPONS

In the early days of the Vietnam War, the Vietcong were equipped only with primitive rifles. These had been handed down from father to son or captured from the French. They also often used homemade ammunition. Gunpowder was made from bat manure mixed with ashes from burned tree bark. This was packed in old gun shell casings behind small stone pebbles. When such crude shells were fired, the stone pebbles were as deadly at close range as steel or lead shotgun pellets.

Shortly before the United States entered the war, the Vietcong captured a great many American-made rifles from ARVN troops. But by the time the first American soldiers ar-

*Americans and South Vietnamese
slosh through
rice fields in search of guerrillas.*

rived in Vietnam, all the Vietcong had been supplied with an excellent new Russian rifle called the AK-47.

The AK-47 was a sturdy, dependable rifle that came to be as highly prized by the Americans as it was by the Vietcong. In fact Americans preferred it to their own M-16, which they often referred to as the "Mattel toy" rifle. The M-16 was frequently inaccurate. Its mechanism jammed if only a few grains of sand got into it. And its plastic stock would break if it was banged sharply against a rock. The barrel of the M-16 burned out if the gun were fired for any length of time. The AK-47, on the other hand, stood up under any and all combat conditions.

PRIMARY LESSONS
IN JUNGLE WARFARE

When American ground troops first went into action in Vietnam, they were easily ambushed by the Vietcong. For one thing the VC could always hear the Americans coming through the jungle. They had not yet learned the need for absolute silence while out on patrol.

Inexperienced American infantrymen going into battle sometimes created their own casualties. This happened because they carried hand grenades behind them on their belts or slung across their backs. Twigs from stout tree branches occasionally caught on the grenades. This resulted in the grenade trigger-pins being pulled, causing the grenades to explode. The grunts soon learned to carry their grenades as the VC did—on a sling across their chests.

ADVANCED U.S. FIREPOWER
AND AIR POWER

What the Americans lacked in jungle fighting skills they tried to make up for in firepower and other advanced weaponry.

There was little doubt that the United States military forces both on land and in the air were far superior to the North Vietnamese.

For one thing, American tanks and heavy guns could destroy whole Vietnamese villages in a few minutes. This was done when such villages were thought to be occupied by Vietcong snipers and bands of guerrillas. However, as soon as such attacks began, the Vietcong escaped from the villages into the nearby jungle. These escapes were usually made through long, narrow tunnels that they had dug from the dirt floors of the villages' thatched huts into the middle of the jungle. Destroying as many such tunnels as possible soon became one of the reasons for American attacks on innocent-looking villages. The fact that women and children often were killed in such attacks caused many Vietnamese civilians to hate and fear the Americans. On the other hand, if civilians did not cooperate with the Vietcong and allow them to live in their villages, they were often shot by the Vietcong. This constant killing of civilians was one of the more brutal tragedies of the Vietnam War.

When the jungle continued to defeat American combat efforts by hiding the enemy, U.S. commanders decided to destroy the jungle. This was done by spraying huge areas with a chemical spray that killed the leaves on the trees. This spray was spread by low-flying U.S. aircraft. The trouble with this effort was that it was almost too successful. It killed not only all of the trees over thousands of square miles, but also all the rice and other crops grown in the area.

Like the French before them, the Americans soon found that their superior manpower and firepower made it possible to control the Vietnamese towns and cities. But they could not control the countryside. Instead of trying to control the countryside, the United States used big fleets of helicopters to

carry troops and supplies between towns and cities. They also used helicopters, or "choppers," to carry men into battle and casualties back to hospitals in Saigon. Helicopters were so widely used that the Vietnam conflict soon became known as the "Chopper War."

Nothing the Americans and their ARVN allies did in South Vietnam, however, seemed to bring the war any closer to a conclusion. And it should be remembered that the ARVN or South Vietnamese soldiers continued to play a major role right along with the Americans in fighting the war. Although American newspaper, radio, and television reporters seldom mentioned the fact, ARVN casualties were usually higher than American casualties.

STEPPED-UP AIR WAR
AGAINST NORTH VIETNAM

When the war in South Vietnam seemed to have come to a standstill, the aerial bombing of North Vietnam was waged with increased fury. The planes used in this effort were the huge American B-52s of the Strategic Air Force. A hundred or more planes took part in each raid. Most raids were launched from the island of Guam in the Pacific Ocean.

Each B-52 carried thirty tons (27 metric tons) of bombs. Three B-52 bombers always flew together in V-formation. Thus each trio of planes could drop ninety tons (81½ metric tons) of bombs on the target all at once. Some planes also carried

U.S. Air Force planes spray
chemical defoliants on
a South Vietnamese jungle.

Choppers were used extensively in the war to carry men into battle.

phosphorous bombs. These started huge fires in the rubble of houses and factories that had already been destroyed, or burned down structures that were still standing.

The B-52s did cause great destruction in Hanoi, but the raids only seemed to strengthen the will of Ho Chi Minh and his people to continue the fight. What was more, the North Vietnamese were by no means unable to strike back at the American bombers.

By now, the North Vietnamese were being supplied with excellent fighter aircraft by the Russians. Called MIGs, these Russian-made fighter planes were every bit as good as the American F-105 Thunderchief fighters that accompanied the B-52s on their bombing missions. But the most effective North Vietnamese defense against the B-52 raids was the so-called SAM. SAM stood for surface-to-air missile. This electronic anti-aircraft device was a kind of aerial torpedo-bomb. After it was launched, it automatically found its way to its target through a built-in guidance system. The SAMs and the radio-operated anti-aircraft guns that guarded the SAM sites were also made by the Russians.

By the late 1960s it had become all too clear to President Johnson and his military leaders that the war in Vietnam was not going to be won quickly or easily. There even began to be some doubt about whether the United States could win it at all. Most serious was the fact that civilians in America were beginning to react strongly against the war. Those most violently opposed to the war seemed to be the nation's young people. It was these young people who were going to have to fight in the war if it was going to continue.

TROUBLE ON
TWO FRONTS

By the end of 1966, there were almost 400,000 American troops in Vietnam. Most of these were young "civilian soldiers" or draftees. Few wanted to be in the armed services at all. Fewer still wanted to be in Vietnam. But the national draft law said that all young men between the ages of eighteen and thirty-five had to sign up for military service. At twenty-one they could be drafted into the armed services. College students, however, were not drafted as long as they had passing grades in their studies.

When the Vietnam War began, there was little objection to the draft law. It was like the law that had been in effect during World War II and the Korean War and people were used to it. But as the casualties increased in Vietnam, young people began to rebel against being drafted. In 1965, these casualties (killed, wounded, and missing in action) totaled 2,500. The next year they grew to 33,000. In 1967 they numbered 80,000. By 1968 they had passed the 125,000 mark. As the casualties grew, so did the number of men who were drafted. Draft calls were about 5,000 men a month in 1965. Soon, however, they reached 50,000 men a month, where they remained until 1969.

The fact that college students were not drafted seemed unfair to many young men. Poor youths who could not afford to go to college had no choice but to go into the armed forces. Since there were so many poor black youths, the draft was especially unfair to them. Spanish-Americans and members of other poor minority groups were also treated un-fairly in the draft.

But it was not the poor draftees who began to rebel against the Vietnam War. Instead, it was college students. As the war dragged on, many such students feared they would soon get out of college and have to go to war rather than to work. Others claimed that they did not believe in war in general and the Vietnam War in particular. The United States, they said, had no right to be killing people in Vietnam.

These young anti-war students showed their disapproval of the draft in various ways. Some burned their draft cards at public meetings. Others marched in parades carrying anti-war signs and chanting anti-war slogans. Soon a law was passed that made the burning of draft cards a criminal of-fense. In addition, the government ruled that all young men taking part in anti-war protests should be immediately drafted. But still the protests continued and even seemed to grow in size and number.

DRAFT EVADERS
AND DESERTERS

Many young American men decided that the only way to get out of being drafted was to leave the United States. By 1967 more than 15,000 American draft evaders were living in To-ronto, Canada, and Stockholm, Sweden.

Some members of the U.S. military forces also decided to leave or desert their units before they could be sent to Vietnam. These military deserters numbered only a few thou-sand men. But when they left their combat units they weak-ened the will-to-fight of many other young soldiers and draft-ees. They also strengthened the will of others to evade the draft. Most of the military deserters joined the groups of draft evaders in Canada and Sweden.

THE KILLINGS
AT KENT STATE

Student protests against the draft and the war in Vietnam sometimes ended in tragedy. The worst such tragedy took place at Kent State University in Ohio in the spring of 1970.

For several days Kent students had been holding anti-war rallies. Shouting, "One, two, three, four, we don't want to go to war," they marched across the campus carrying burning torches. One of these rallies got out of hand and torches were thrown into a building used by the ROTC (Reserve Officers Training Corps). The building burned to the ground.

To prevent the student demonstrations from becoming riots and spreading into the town of Kent, the National Guard was called out. At first the trouble seemed to be over. But then what started out as a peaceful anti-war rally on the campus Commons ended in bloody tragedy.

The Guardsmen ordered the students to break up the rally. Their response was to throw several rocks at the Guardsmen. Cans of tear gas were then thrown at the students. The students threw the cans back along with more rocks. The Guardsmen retreated a short distance. Then several of them turned and opened fire with M-1 rifles on the students. Within seconds, thirteen students had been shot. Four of them, one of whom was an ROTC cadet, were killed.

WINNING THE HEARTS AND
MINDS OF THE VIETNAMESE

President Johnson's administration also faced serious trouble on the South Vietnamese home front. Much of this trou-

Kent State students disperse as National Guardsmen fire tear gas into the crowd. Just moments from now, four students will be shot to death by the guardsmen.

Searching South Vietnamese villages for Viet-cong hideouts became a major activity during the war in Vietnam. Many of the villages were destroyed simply to rout the enemy.

ble was caused by the methods used for winning the war by the U.S. top military commander, General William C. Westmoreland.

Attempts to bomb the Vietcong from the air often resulted in the deaths of many South Vietnamese civilians. It was hard to convince the relatives of those who had been killed in such air raids that the Americans were on the side of the South Vietnamese.

In addition, civilians were forced to leave any area that was suspected of being occupied by the Vietcong. The area was then called a "Free Fire Zone." This meant that every village in the Free Fire Zone could be destroyed by artillery or aerial bombardment.

The Vietnamese civilians became angry when they had to leave their home villages. They believed that the spirits of their ancestors still lived in them. Once these villages were destroyed the Vietnamese civilians felt they no longer had a true home.

But General Westmoreland's forces continued to create Free Fire Zones as the best method for killing the Vietcong. The fact that most of the Vietcong had left a village by the time it was destroyed did not seem to make any difference.

Village life in South Vietnam was also destroyed by an American attempt to "win the hearts and minds of the people." This program was supposed to convince all South Vietnamese that Democracy was better than Communism. To protect the South Vietnamese people in rural areas from attacks by the Vietcong, they were taken out of their villages and placed in large camps, where they were guarded by ARVN troops. In these camps the South Vietnamese were given classroom talks about what great improvements in their way of life there would be when the war was won and all of Vietnam became one big democracy.

But most of the South Vietnamese farmers did not care what kind of government they lived under as long as they were allowed to live in peace in their own villages. They felt like prisoners after being removed from their home villages and forced to live in the huge central camps. In addition, there seemed to be very little democratic freedom under the present South Vietnamese government. Every President since Diem had continued to act like a dictator. There still had been no free elections, and it didn't look like there would be any.

It was finally agreed by both U.S. and South Vietnamese leaders that probably the best way of winning the hearts and minds of the people would be to attend to the business of winning the war. President Johnson decided that what was needed was a new South Vietnamese President. General Khanh, who had succeeded Diem, had been a failure. Several others who had followed Khanh had also been failures. But now, Johnson thought, the ideal new President had been found. He was General Nguyen Van Thieu.

Van Thieu, who became President of South Vietnam in 1967, had been one of the generals who overthrew Diem. He was a popular national hero. Van Thieu thought the future looked bright. And, despite serious troubles both at home and abroad, so did President Johnson.

Nguyen Van Thieu

THE TET OFFENSIVE

The future looked bright to Presidents Johnson and Van Thieu because, for the first time, the United States and South Vietnam now seemed to be winning the war.

In the early spring of 1967, General Westmoreland's forces launched an all-out attack in an area just north of Saigon, called the Iron Triangle. It had long been occupied by large numbers of Vietcong. The combined American-ARVN attack drove all of the Vietcong out of the Iron Triangle.

A few weeks later a second Allied attack struck a Vietcong headquarters near Cambodia. This offensive also seemed successful when all of the Vietcong under attack fled into Cambodia.

But there were two flaws in the apparent victories. Within a few months the Vietcong had returned in full force both to the headquarters area near Cambodia and to the Iron Triangle. In addition, thousands of South Vietnamese civilians were forced to flee the Iron Triangle area when it was declared a Free Fire Zone just before the Allied attack. These civilians had no place to go but into Saigon. There they found little food and few places to live except in the streets.

But Westmoreland made no mention of these problems when President Johnson asked him to return to the United States in late 1967 and report on the progress of the war.

"I have never been more encouraged since I have been in Vietnam," Westmoreland told a national television audience. He even predicted that it would not be long before American troops could begin coming home from Vietnam.

Privately, however, Westmoreland told Johnson that more U.S. troops would be needed to win the war. Reluctantly, Johnson agreed. But he put a limit of 525,000 on the number of men he would allow to be shipped to Vietnam. Within a few months this ceiling would be raised to near the 550,000 mark.

Meanwhile, Ho Chi Minh and General Giap were preparing a very special way to welcome in the new year of 1968.

At the beginning of the New Year in Vietnam there is a national holiday called *Tet*. For several days there are parades and parties and religious worship. Both the North and South Vietnamese thought that fighting would stop during the Tet holiday. There had always been such a truce in the past.

But Ho Chi Minh and General Giap had other ideas. This year they planned to pretend to go along with the Tet truce. Then, when everybody in South Vietnam was least expecting it, the North Vietnamese regular army and the Vietcong would launch an all-out offensive.

THE TET OFFENSIVE
BUILD-UP

When General Westmoreland returned to South Vietnam from the United States he began to get reports that the enemy was getting ready for a big offensive. This did not bother him and his aides too much. In fact, they thought it might even be a good thing if such an offensive took place. That would bring the enemy's guerrilla forces together into one main body of troops that the Americans and ARVN troops could destroy. But not even General Westmoreland thought that the enemy would launch a major attack during the Tet holiday.

Because the Vietnamese calendar is unlike ours, the new

year usually starts at a different time in Vietnam than it does in the United States. In 1968 the Tet New Year holiday was to begin on January 30.

To fool the Americans and South Vietnamese, Ho Chi Minh agreed that there should be no fighting between January 27 and February 3. Ho Chi Minh also said that he was willing to hold peace talks during the truce. He would only do this, he added, if the Americans stopped the aerial bombing of North Vietnam for several weeks before Tet. Eagerly, the United States agreed. This, of course, gave General Giap time to build up his troop strength for the big offensive. Secretly, Ho Chi Minh and Giap agreed that the Tet offensive would get under way right in the middle of the Tet truce, on January 30.

In the days and weeks before Tet, General Giap quietly went about the job of strengthening the Vietcong forces in South Vietnam. Down the Ho Chi Minh Trail and through the jungles on both sides of the DMZ moved North Vietnamese troops and supplies. Troop reinforcements were spread everywhere in South Vietnam including Saigon itself.

THE TET OFFENSIVE
BEGINS

At dawn on January 30, 1968, the Vietcong suddenly struck at well over a hundred cities and major towns throughout South Vietnam. At most so-called strongpoints there were few defenders. Almost all of the ARVN troops were home for the Tet holiday. American commanders had also taken advantage of the truce to give their men some time off. Only skeleton staffs were kept on duty at most headquarters.

In Saigon the American Embassy and South Vietnamese Presidential Palace were both attacked, badly damaged, and their few defenders killed. Other government buildings and airplanes at the Saigon airport were also destroyed.

South of Saigon in the Mekong Delta region, several ARVN headquarters were captured. A major American camp at Cam Ranh Bay and the key American airfield at Da Nang were both heavily attacked. At Da Nang numerous American airplanes were destroyed.

One of the main goals of the Tet offensive was the capture of Khe Sanh, an important American base just south of the DMZ. General Giap sent a force of 20,000 crack North Vietnamese regulars and veteran Vietcong against this strongpoint. But the 10,000 U.S. Marines at Khe Sanh were on the alert. They drove off the attackers with heavy losses and prepared to counterattack.

When General Giap saw that Khe Sanh could not be quickly captured, he ordered some of his troops to surround it. Others he ordered to move down the peninsula to Hue, one of the oldest and most sacred cities in South Vietnam. Hue quickly fell to the onrushing enemy.

THE AMERICANS AND
ARVN STRIKE BACK

Within hours after the Tet offensive began, General Westmoreland began to rally his Allied forces to strike back. The Vietcong were quickly driven from Saigon and order was restored there. The Mekong Delta area was also retaken in a few days. Elsewhere, however, the enemy stubbornly resisted all counterattacks.

Some of the most stubborn enemy resistance was at Hue. There it took a month for ARVN forces and U.S. Marines aided by aerial bombardment to recapture the city. When the enemy was finally driven out of Hue, three-quarters of the

city lay in ruins. By the time the seventy-two-day siege at Khe Sanh was broken, that city too was all but destroyed.

Gradually, throughout South Vietnam all of the towns and cities captured by the North Vietnamese and Vietcong in the Tet offensive were recaptured. Then it was time to total up the casualties, or "butcher's bill" as the military call it. The butcher's bill was a big one.

It was estimated that some 165,000 civilians had been killed in South Vietnam. Another two million civilians had been driven from their homes. Once again many of these refugees fled into Saigon. ARVN and American casualties came to 4,200 killed and 16,000 wounded. Vietcong and North Vietnamese regular army casualties were much larger. They were estimated at 45,000 killed and 100,000 wounded. There were also some 7,000 enemy prisoners of war, which was a rarity. The Vietcong seldom allowed themselves to be taken prisoner, choosing instead to fight to the death.

REACTION ON
THE HOME FRONT

Both General Westmoreland and President Johnson claimed that the Tet offensive had resulted in a defeat for the North Vietnamese and the Vietcong. It was actually an Allied victory, they claimed. As far as a comparison between the number of casualties on both sides was concerned, this claim

*Two small Vietnamese girls
in the village of Hue walk in the
rubble that was once their home.
Much of Hue was destroyed
during the Tet offensive.*

was true. But the great number of enemy dead, or the "body count" as it was called, made little difference to the American people.

The United States, both Westmoreland and Johnson had said, was winning the war. If this were true, how could the enemy suddenly stage an attack that almost overran the whole of South Vietnam? Vermont Senator George D. Aiken spoke for the entire nation when he said, "If the Tet offensive was a failure, I hope the Vietcong never have a major success."

President Johnson knew that he must have the support of the American people if he were going to continue to lead the United States to victory in the war in Vietnam. He was beginning to realize that he did not have that support. He also faced a barrage of criticism about his conduct of the war from the American press and television. In March of 1968 Johnson announced that he would not run for re-election.

But the national election would not be held until the fall. And a new President would not take office until January of 1969. Meanwhile, the war would go on.

President Johnson's next move was to recall General Westmoreland from Vietnam. He replaced him with General Creighton W. Abrams. Abrams had been second in command to Westmoreland. On taking over as the new top military commander, Abrams said he "would not stop short of a complete victory in Vietnam."

General Abrams was welcomed to his new job by another major offensive by General Giap. This was not as big nor as successful as the Tet offensive. But it clearly showed that victory for the United States and South Vietnam was far from certain or even in sight. On June 23, 1968, the war in Vietnam became the longest war in United States history.

*President Johnson, on national television,
tells of his decision not to run for re-election.*

NIXON ELECTED PRESIDENT

When Johnson decided not to run for re-election, his Vice President, Hubert H. Humphrey, was nominated by the Democrats as their presidential candidate. He was opposed by Republican Richard M. Nixon. Nixon was a former U.S. Senator and Vice President under President Eisenhower. He promised to end the draft, bring the American troops home from Vietnam, and end the war.

Nixon did not say just how he planned to achieve these goals. Nor did he say how he would achieve "Peace with Honor." Nevertheless, on this slogan he was elected President on November 5, 1968, to succeed Lyndon Johnson. Unfortunately, Nixon's "Peace with Honor" would in the end turn out to be "Defeat with Dishonor."

VIETNAMIZATION
OF THE WAR

Like the Presidents before him, Nixon had no intention of losing the Vietnam War. But he still wanted to win it as soon as possible. Like President Johnson, Nixon also knew he must have public support to carry on the conflict. His plan for getting both public support and quick victory was called "Vietnamization."

Vietnamization simply meant that most of the fighting against North Vietnam and the Vietcong would now be done by the South Vietnamese. Gradually, all United States ground troops would be pulled out of South Vietnam. But the United States would continue to give South Vietnam all of the money and military supplies needed by the ARVN forces to fight alone. The United States would also continue to give air support to ARVN ground forces.

Initially, Nixon's plan looked exactly like Johnson's at the start of the war. But there was one major difference. Johnson had gradually sent more and more American troops into battle. Nixon promised to reverse that flow.

Nixon had long thought that the draft was the main reason for the anti-war movement in the United States. He planned to reduce draft calls and then eliminate the draft entirely. By now more than 33,000 Americans had been killed in South Vietnam. This was more men than had been killed in the Korean War. Nixon knew that the public simply would not stand for many more combat deaths.

Nixon announced that by the end of 1969 more than

100,000 U.S. troops would be returned from Vietnam. And all American troops, he said, would be out of Vietnam by 1970 or 1971.

The main problem with Vietnamization was that South Vietnam's President Van Thieu did not think that ARVN forces would be able to do anything but defend South Vietnam. And he was not even sure they could do that all by themselves. Attacking the enemy, Van Thieu said, would be out of the question. So unless something else were done, the bloody war in South Vietnam would drag on indefinitely. Nixon and his foreign policy adviser, Henry Kissinger, agreed. The "something else" they thought would decide the war was Johnson's old solution—a huge increase in the aerial bombardment of North Vietnam.

PEACE TALKS IN
PARIS FOLLOW DEATH
OF HO CHI MINH

A few months after it began, Nixon's Vietnamization plan looked like it was going to be a great success. On September 3, 1969, Ho Chi Minh died in Hanoi. Shortly afterwards, the North Vietnamese agreed to begin formal peace talks in Paris.

But North Vietnam's decision to sit down at the peace table was misleading. No one knew whether the decision was caused by Ho Chi Minh's death, the threat of increased bombing of North Vietnam, or the gradual withdrawal of U.S. troops. Whatever the reason, U.S. delegates to the peace conference soon found out that North Vietnam's new leaders were as stubborn as the old.

Henry Cabot Lodge and David K. E. Bruce were the United States' peace delegates. The chief North Vietnamese delegate was Le Duc Tho. Speaking for Pham Van Dong, the new

North Vietnamese Premier, Le Duc Tho, told Lodge and Bruce that the United States must get entirely out of the Vietnam war before peace terms could be seriously discussed. In addition, he demanded that Vietnam become one united and independent country. If these demands were not met, Le Duc Tho said, there was no point in carrying on any further discussions.

What now became clear to U.S. leaders was that North Vietnam was simply stalling for time until the United States withdrew all of its troops from the war. Then the North Vietnamese would make Vietnam one "independent" country by overrunning South Vietnam. Although the peace talks continued, there were few signs that they would bring any quick results.

In an attempt to force a decision at the peace table, the United States renewed its aerial bombardment of North Vietnam. And using the large number of American forces still at his command, General Abrams also stepped up the ground campaign against the Vietcong. Abrams believed that the Tet offensive had seriously hurt the Vietcong, because once again they were refusing to meet his troops in face-to-face battle. Instead they had gone back to their guerrilla-style warfare.

The Vietcong guerrillas were especially active in areas near the Cambodian border. This had been so all during the war. VC guerrillas would engage in hit-and-run attacks against American or ARVN forces. Then they would escape from any counterattacks by fleeing across the border into Cambodia. There they were safe because Cambodia was not fighting in the war. It was a neutral country. The United States did not want to cross Cambodia's borders and destroy its neutrality. But under President Nixon the United States changed its mind about this.

THE INVASION OF CAMBODIA

Cambodia's ruler was Prince Norodom Sihanouk. Prince Sihanouk had been mainly responsible for keeping his country out of the war. But early in 1970 Sihanouk was overthrown by one of his army generals, Lon Nol. When Lon Nol seized control of the Cambodian government, U.S. military leaders saw they had a chance to invade Cambodia and drive out the North Vietnamese who were hiding there. Lon Nol was a violent anti-Communist and made it clear he would not object to such American action.

The places where the North Vietnamese hid were called sanctuaries. Although the United States had never admitted it, hundreds of secret American air raids had already been made against these hiding places. But the raids had had little effect on the enemy. Military leaders insisted that the only thing that would succeed was to invade Cambodia with infantry and drive the Vietcong from the sanctuaries. President Nixon and Henry Kissinger agreed.

On April 29, 1970, the day the invasion of Cambodia began, Nixon told the American people: "For five years neither the United States nor South Vietnam has moved against the sanctuaries because we did not want to violate the territory of a neutral nation." Nixon made no mention of the secret air raids that had already violated Cambodia's neutrality and had also failed in their purpose. The Vietcong, according to the President, had made it impossible for this "hands-off policy" to continue. They had to be driven out of their Cambodian sanctuaries if Vietnamization was to succeed.

As soon as the invasion began, what Prince Sihanouk had feared immediately began to happen. The North Vietnamese moved into Cambodia in great numbers to occupy and "defend" the country. The United States had forced Cambodia into the war.

Reaction in the United States was equally swift and equally violent. The most serious and widespread anti-war demonstrations to date broke out. The killings at Kent State University took place during this time.

The nation's lawmakers were also angered by Nixon's and Kissinger's spreading of the war into a neutral country. The U.S. Senate passed a resolution that American troops must be withdrawn from Cambodia and that aerial bombing of the sanctuaries must stop.

THE INVASION OF LAOS

By the summer of 1970 American troops had all been withdrawn from Cambodia. But now the U.S. Congress feared that the Nixon administration might attempt to invade Laos. Since a part of the Ho Chi Minh Trail ran through Laos, the U.S. military had also long wanted to take over that country. To prevent this, Congress passed a resolution saying that no American troops could be used there. The Gulf of Tonkin Resolution was also repealed. This took away most of the special war-making powers that had been granted President Johnson and that were still in effect.

But the invasion of Laos took place anyway.

Early in 1971, some 16,000 ARVN troops moved into Laos. Although they were not accompanied by American troops, they were given heavy U.S. air support. But air support was not enough. Within a matter of weeks the ARVN invasion of Laos had proved to be a disaster. Vietcong infantry supported by North Vietnamese tanks and artillery inflicted huge casualties on the invaders.

With a loss of some 10,000 men, the ARVN forces withdrew from Laos in March. In addition to battle casualties the South Vietnamese army was now losing thousands of men a month through desertion. These men simply left their combat units and went home.

THE PENTAGON PAPERS

The disaster in Laos caused new demands for the war in Vietnam to be ended with or without victory. These demands reached their peak in June with the publication of what were called "The Pentagon Papers."

The Pentagon is the building in Washington, D.C., that is the headquarters of the U.S. Department of Defense. It is built in the shape of a *pentagon,* which is a Greek word for a five-sided figure.

During most of President Johnson's administration, Robert S. McNamara had been Secretary of Defense. Like Johnson, McNamara had started out as a "hawk," or one who was in favor of America's part in the Vietnam War. But the longer the war went on the less he was in favor of it. Soon he became an outspoken "dove," in favor of America's withdrawal from Vietnam. Finally, in 1968, McNamara resigned as Secretary of Defense.

But before he resigned, McNamara had his staff at the Pentagon prepare a report on just how the United States had become involved in the Vietnam War. McNamara also wanted the report to show how the United States had continued to get more and more deeply involved in the conflict while keeping this knowledge from the American public. All of the Pentagon's secret files dating from the end of World War II right up to the present were used.

One of the people who worked on this report was a young man named Daniel Ellsberg. Like McNamara, Ellsberg had started out the war as a hawk but soon became a dove. He became convinced that the United States was mainly to blame for the Vietnam War. As far as Ellsberg was concerned, the secret Pentagon report proved his point. He thought it should be made public. But because the report was classified as secret its publication was not permitted. Nevertheless, Ellsberg decided to "leak" copies of it to the press.

The Pentagon Papers were first printed in *The New York Times* and then elsewhere. They showed how each U.S. President from Truman through Johnson had gotten the nation more and more deeply involved in Indochina. They also left little doubt that the depth of this involvement had been kept secret. Many undercover U.S. military activities in Vietnam before the Gulf of Tonkin incident were disclosed. The combat activities of the Green Berets and the secret operations of the U.S. Central Intelligence Agency (CIA) were now made public for the first time. Detailed accounts of the secret aerial bombardment of North Vietnam, Laos, and Cambodia showed that the United States had actually been waging an undeclared war while the American public thought only ARVN forces were involved.

The Pentagon Papers came down especially hard on the Johnson administration. They showed how President Johnson told the public one thing and did another. When he told news people that no American troops would be sent to Vietnam, orders had already been given for just such troop shipments. The CIA had reported that the aerial bombardment of Hanoi only made North Vietnam more determined than ever to continue the war. Yet such bombardments had continued in order to force the North Vietnamese to bow before America's superior military might.

Most damaging of all to the Johnson administration was the doubt the Pentagon Papers cast on the truth of the events in the Gulf of Tonkin. Much evidence showed that this incident had been manufactured by the United States to provoke a shooting war.

Despite the fact that the Pentagon Papers were not critical of his administration, President Nixon tried to prevent their being published. He and his aides thought that if they were published a similar secret report on the Nixon undercover war efforts might also one day become public. Daniel Ellsberg was arrested, and a Federal judge issued a temporary ban on the Pentagon Papers' publication. But Ellsberg was quickly freed on bail, and the United States Supreme Court said the Pentagon Papers could be printed. Eventually Ellsberg was cleared of all charges.

Within a few weeks the sensation caused by the Pentagon Papers died down. But they would eventually prove to be the handwriting on the wall spelling the end of the war in Vietnam as well as the end of the Nixon administration.

PEACE WITHOUT HONOR

In the spring of 1972, North Vietnam launched another major military offensive against South Vietnam. United States troop strength was now down to 70,000 men. They fought heroically alongside the ARVN troops to prevent the whole of South Vietnam from being overrun. Massive U.S. air power was also used to stop the advance on all fronts. Nevertheless, the Vietcong moved to within artillery distance of Saigon before they faltered.

In the fall of 1972, the North Vietnamese said they were willing to resume peace talks in Paris. Nixon wanted peace to be agreed upon by November because he was running for re-election to the presidency. The man he was running against was Democratic Senator George McGovern of South Dakota. McGovern was a well-known dove and was campaigning for "Peace Now in Vietnam."

For a time the Paris peace talks stalled because the North Vietnamese insisted that South Vietnam's President Van Thieu must be removed from office. But in mid-October Henry Kissinger persuaded Le Duc Tho to withdraw this demand. Kissinger then proudly announced: "Peace is at hand!" The Kissinger announcement helped Nixon win a landslide victory over McGovern in November.

Unfortunately, no cease-fire followed Nixon's re-election. President Van Thieu refused to go along with the peace terms. He publicly accused the United States of selling out South Vietnam in a peace-at-any-price deal.

The North Vietnamese further complicated the peace agreement by refusing to agree to the immediate release of

*Nixon and Kissinger discuss
the stalled peace talks in Paris.*

the Americans they were holding as prisoners of war. Hundreds of these prisoners were in hidden North Vietnamese camps.

NIXON'S
CHRISTMAS PRESENT
FOR HANOI

Nixon's angry response to the new stalling tactics was to order the saturation bombing of North Vietnam. Hanoi was bombed twenty-four hours a day for days on end. Hanoi's harbor, Haiphong, was also blockaded and bombed. Until now, the United States had been especially careful about bombing Haiphong harbor or railroads and bridges north of Hanoi near the Chinese border. There were always Russian ships in the harbor. If these were hit, Russia might actively enter the war. If American bombs north of Hanoi went astray and landed in China, China might also actively enter the war. Now, however, Nixon threw caution to the winds, and the most savage aerial attack of the entire war was unleashed on these formerly forbidden targets.

Nixon's gamble paid off. China's and Russia's reaction to the bombing was to secretly urge North Vietnam to end the war. Meanwhile, the U.S. Congress was also preparing legislation that would put an end to all U.S. aerial bombardment in Vietnam. Hanoi's response came shortly after Christmas in 1972. Premier Pham Van Dong agreed to a cease-fire.

The cease-fire agreement that was supposed to end all hostilities in Vietnam was signed by Le Duc Tho and Henry Kissinger on January 27, 1973. By spring all of the American combat troops had been returned to the United States. Only a few hundred Marine guards remained on duty at the U.S. Embassy in Saigon. Between February and April, some six hun-

*A cease-fire agreement is finally reached.
Here, Kissinger and Le Duc Tho are
seen initialing the official document.*

dred prisoners of war were released by the North Vietnamese. Several hundred others soon followed.

But the cease-fire did not end hostilities in Vietnam. Soon fighting had spread throughout Laos and Cambodia in what amounted to an Indochinese civil war. The cease-fire was broken by both sides. North Vietnam continued to send soldiers into South Vietnam to support the Vietcong. The United States continued to give money, military supplies, and aircraft to South Vietnam. American aircraft were used on raids throughout Indochina.

Finally, in August of 1973, the Nixon administration was forced to end its support of all military efforts in Indochina when the U.S. Congress cut off all funds to pay for them. In South Vietnam, President Van Thieu and his ARVN forces were left to fight on alone against the North Vietnamese. Laos quickly became a North Vietnamese puppet state. And in Cambodia, Premier Lon Nol was also abandoned to his fate. Lon Nol's government was being threatened not only by the North Vietnamese but also by revolutionary forces within his own country.

Both Van Thieu and Lon Nol were briefly encouraged when a new U.S. President, Gerald R. Ford, took office. Vice President Ford succeeded Nixon as President when several scandals at home forced Nixon to resign in 1974. But Ford's appeal for more war funds fell on deaf ears. The U.S. Congress refused the new President's request.

THE WATERGATE AFFAIR

Nixon had resigned from office because of what was called the "Watergate Affair." The Watergate Affair actually grew out of the war in Vietnam and Daniel Ellsberg's release of the Pentagon Papers.

After Ellsberg leaked the Pentagon Papers to the press, Nixon's aides broke into Ellsberg's psychiatrist's office in Los Angeles. These burglars were called the "Plumbers' Unit" because they were supposed to fix the leak of any more government secrets. The Plumbers hoped to find information about Ellsberg that might hurt his reputation. They found nothing.

Later, when Nixon was running for President in 1972, a second Plumbers' Unit went into action. It burglarized the national headquarters of the Democratic party. These headquarters were located in the Watergate building in Washington, D.C. There the Plumbers tapped the phones and planted electronic "bugs" in the offices of the people who were running the presidential campaign against Nixon. The phone taps and "bugs" would let Nixon's aides listen in on their opponents' plans. The Plumbers were also trying to steal written Democratic campaign plans.

The Plumbers' break-in at Watergate was interrupted by an alert night watchman, and the burglars were caught. But they were not immediately connected with the White House. It was not until many months later that the American public learned that President Nixon and his aides knew about the Watergate break-in shortly after it happened. The public also learned during a dramatic Senate investigation of the break-in that the President had tried to cover up his knowledge of the burglary. As a result of the Watergate Affair, Nixon resigned as President on August 8, 1974. He was immediately succeeded by Gerald Ford.

THE FINAL ACT

The United States' role in the war in Vietnam actually ended when Congress refused President Ford's request for more military funds. But the tragedy of Vietnam and the rest of Indochina continued without our aid.

In January of 1975, the North Vietnamese mounted a massive armored attack that crossed the DMZ into South Vietnam. By early spring, the North Vietnamese had moved to the outskirts of Saigon. On April 21, President Van Thieu resigned and fled into exile. On April 30, the new South Vietnamese President, General Duong Van Minh surrendered Saigon.

News cameramen were still on duty at the American Embassy as the North Vietnamese took over Saigon. Soon television viewers in the United States and around the world were witnesses to the final tragic scenes in the first war America had ever lost. American rescue helicopters landed on the roof of the embassy as well as on the embassy grounds to carry U.S. officials and the last of the U.S. Marine guard to safety. These helicopters flew out to sea where the U.S. Navy rescue vessels waited.

A few South Vietnamese top government officials and army officers were also rescued by the American helicopters. Others flew to safety from airfields elsewhere in South Vietnam or escaped by sea. The rest were left behind. In the final hours of the rescue operation many South Vietnamese civilians tried to climb the fences surrounding the U.S. Embassy grounds but were beaten off by American guards.

CASUALTIES IN THE WAR
During the course of the war a total of more than 2½ million Americans served in Vietnam. American military forces reached a peak strength of 543,000 men in 1969. Some 46,000 Americans were killed in combat, and 300,000 were wounded. Most of these casualties were suffered by the infantry soldiers. Another 10,000 men died of non-combat related acci-

dents or illnesses. About 1,300 Americans were listed as missing in action. The draft was officially ended in June of 1973. The cost of the war for the United States has been estimated at more than $110 billion.

More than 200,000 South Vietnamese soldiers were killed and about 500,000 were wounded in the war. According to official estimates 500,000 South Vietnamese civilians were killed and as many as a million were wounded.

North Vietnamese casualties were estimated to be higher, although the accuracy of the figures still is in doubt. Up to one million North Vietnamese soldiers were killed and as many as three million were wounded. The number of North Vietnamese civilian deaths is unknown.

In Laos and Cambodia no records of war casualties were kept, so it is impossible to know how many people were killed and wounded there while America was in the war.

In all, total war dead have been estimated at more than two million. Total cost of the war is unknown but has been estimated at up to $500 billion.

AFTERMATH IN VIETNAM

When North Vietnam overran South Vietnam many Americans feared there would be a "blood bath" in South Vietnam. This did not happen. Saigon was renamed Ho Chi Minh city, and the North Vietnamese took over the running of the government. There were no national elections, but the whole of Vietnam was united in what amounted to a Communist dictatorship.

Also fearing a blood bath, many South Vietnamese civilians escaped by boat and sought refuge elsewhere. Some South Vietnamese officials and army officers who did not escape by air or sea were killed or simply disappeared. But most were made political prisoners. They were sent to "re-education camps," where they were taught Communist ideas about government and the Communist way of life.

In 1977 the United States withdrew its objections to Vietnam becoming a member of the United Nations. Some efforts were also made to normalize relations between the United States and Vietnam. By the early 1980s this had still not occurred. Several things stood in the way. First, many Americans believed that Vietnam had still not returned all prisoners of war nor all of the bodies of U.S. servicemen killed in the war. Second, Hanoi officials claimed that President Nixon had agreed, through Henry Kissinger during the peace talks in 1973, that the United States would give financial aid to help rebuild war-torn Vietnam once the cease-fire agreement was signed. Later U.S. administrations refused to honor the Nixon postwar agreement—if indeed Nixon had ever made it. And third, the United States objected to Vietnam's continued efforts to take over the rest of Indochina.

AFTERMATH IN LAOS AND CAMBODIA

Under Ho Chi Minh, the war in Vietnam had started out as a fight for Vietnamese independence. But this goal began to change during Ho Chi Minh's lifetime. And after Ho's death it became all too clear that the goal of the Vietnamese Communist Party was to gain complete control of all of what had been French Indochina. And this, of course, was exactly what President Eisenhower had feared when he stated his Domino Theory.

Once the North Vietnamese had driven the United States completely out of South Vietnam, in 1975 they turned their attention to Laos. They had little trouble taking over there. A longtime Communist leader in Laos, Prince Souphan-ouvong was put in office as President of the Republic of Laos. He took his orders directly from Communist leaders in Hanoi.

But in Cambodia it was a different story. Lon Nol's regime was ousted by a Cambodian revolutionary named Pol Pot. The country was renamed Kampuchea. Pol Pot refused to take orders from the Vietnamese. In addition, he asked the Chinese for help. Although the Chinese had been the allies of North Vietnam, they did not want the Vietnamese to become too strong an Indochinese empire. Such a mini-empire would be a threat to China's southern border. So the Chinese helped the Cambodians defend themselves against the Vietnamese.

Russia, however, had long been a rival of China. As a result, it backed Vietnam in its efforts to gain control of Cambodia. In January of 1979 the Vietnamese Communists supported by Russian military aid mounted a full-scale effort to take over all of Cambodia. Soon Russian aid amounted to $1 billion a year.

The following month, when it looked like the Vietnamese were about to destroy Pol Pot's Cambodian forces, the Chinese invaded Vietnam. This invasion lasted only five weeks. Its purpose, the Chinese said, was "to teach the Vietnamese a lesson." But the Vietnamese did not learn their lesson. They continued to try to take over Cambodia. And Pol Pot's forces continued to resist.

Pol Pot's forces were called the Khmer Rouge. The Khmer Rouge wanted to turn back history's clock in Cambodia and recreate a society like that of the ancient Khmer nation. To turn back the clock they turned into mad terrorists. They killed anybody who was the least bit educated. The lives of anybody who could read were in danger. Even people who wore glasses were not safe from destruction. As a result of this purge, countless thousands of native Cambodians were killed or driven from their homeland.

One of the excuses the Vietnamese used for taking over Cambodia was to rescue the people from the Khmer Rouge. But the Vietnamese were equally brutal. Under the Khmer Rouge the Cambodian economy had been ruined, and those people who hadn't been killed or driven from the country soon began to starve. When various nations around the world offered to send relief shipments of food, the Vietnamese at first refused to accept the food. They claimed it would fall into the hands of the Khmer Rouge. By 1980 it was estimated that at least half of Cambodia's eight million people had been killed by the Khmer Rouge, starved to death under the Vietnamese, or had fled the country.

THE BOAT PEOPLE

Many Cambodians fled into nearby Thailand. Others, like the refugees from South Vietnam, somehow managed to obtain primitive boats and fled to countries throughout Southeast Asia. These thousands of Indochinese "boat people" caused concern throughout the world. In time, a limited number of them found permanent homes in Europe and the United States. World relief agencies also were able to get food and medical supplies into Thailand for the refugees.

The half-million refugees who fled into Thailand caused serious problems for that country. First the Khmer Rouge and then the Vietnamese threatened to invade Thailand if it did not stop accepting refugees. The Vietnamese also accused the Thais of permitting the Chinese to ship military supplies through Thailand to aid Pol Pot and his Khmer Rouge. There were several serious border incidents that threatened to flare into full-scale war against Thailand. And if this happened, the United States was pledged to go to the aid of Thailand. This, of course, would bring China and Russia into the conflict. Thus, the Indochinese problem continued to be a major threat to peace among three of the world's big powers—Russia, China, and the United States.

GUERRILLA WARFARE
AGAINST THE VIETNAMESE

By early 1980 the Vietnamese Communists had installed their own puppet premier, Heng Samrin, in Cambodia. Although they had some 200,000 troops in Cambodia, the Vietnamese had not been able to bring the country under complete military control. Pol Pot's forces numbered only 30,000 men. Their central stronghold was in the Cardamom Mountains in southwestern Cambodia. The Vietnamese were unable to dislodge the Khmer Rouge from this stronghold. Neither could they get them to come out and fight in a face-to-face battle and thus risk a final defeat. The Vietnamese were faced with the bitter fate of having to take a dose of their own medicine.

Outnumbered though they were, Pol Pot's Khmer Rouge were seasoned guerrillas. They rallied forth from their mountain strongholds in small guerrilla bands, made deadly hit-and-run attacks, and then disappeared back into the mountains. Unable to defeat the Khmer Rouge, the Vietnamese were also unwilling to leave the country and turn it over to them. The Vietnamese were bogged down in Cambodia in a seemingly endless guerrilla war just as first the French and then the Americans had been bogged down in Vietnam. Meanwhile, Russia was getting more and more impatient about spending billions of dollars to help an ally in a war it seemed unable to win.

The final outcome in Indochina is as shrouded in mystery as the Cardamom Mountains are shrouded in the clouds that hide the embattled Khmer Rouge. The answer lies somewhere in the future. The world watches and wonders if and when the next domino will fall.

FOR FURTHER READING

Bonds, Ray (ed.). *The Vietnam War.* New York: Crown, 1979.

Fitzgerald, Frances. *Fire in the Lake.* New York: Vintage, 1973, paperback.

Halberstam, David. *The Best and the Brightest.* New York: Fawcett, 1973, paperback.

Kearns, Doris. *Lyndon Johnson and the American Dream.* New York: Signet, 1977, paperback.

Kissinger, Henry. *White House Years.* Boston: Little Brown, 1979.

Lewy, Guenter. *America in Vietnam.* New York: Oxford, 1978.

Manchester, William. *The Glory and the Dream.* New York: Bantam, 1975, paperback.

Moore, Robin. *The Green Berets.* New York: Crown, 1965.

New York Times, The. *The Pentagon Papers.* New York: Bantam, 1971, paperback.

Poole, Peter A. *Dien Bien Phu.* New York: Watts, 1972.

Salisbury, Harrison E. *Behind the Lines—Hanoi.* New York: Harper & Row, 1967, paperback.

Shawcross, William. *Sideshow.* New York: Pocket Books, 1979, paperback.

White, Theodore H. *Breach of Faith: The Fall of Richard Nixon.* New York: Atheneum, 1975.

INDEX

ABOUT THE AUTHOR

Don Lawson is currently editor in chief of the *American Educator's Encyclopedia*, published by United Educators. He is also the author of over twenty books for young people including, most recently for Franklin Watts, *The Picture Life of Ronald Reagan.*